The Magical Twins

A journey Of Light

By: LATONNE ADESANYA

Copyright © 2025 The Magical twins, By: Latonne Adesanya

All rights reserved. This book or any portion thereof may not be reproduced or used in any manner whatsoever without the express written permission of the publisher except for the use of brief quotations in a book review.

The Magical Twins: A Journey of Light"

Meet Zara and Zane, two extraordinary twins with albinism, a special condition that makes their hair, skin, and eyes as white as snow. In their school, they quickly learn that being different can feel a bit tricky at first—but they soon discover that their uniqueness gives them superpowers! With their bright personalities and a world that seems a little more dazzling to them, Zara and Zane embark on an unforgettable adventure. Along the way, they help their classmates see that being different isn't something to hide from—it's something to celebrate. Join these incredible twins as they teach everyone at school that being yourself is the greatest superpower of all!

In a bright and bustling town, there lived two extraordinary twins—Zara and Zane. They were 5 years old, and they were unlike anyone else in their class. Their skin was pale, their hair was as white as snow, and their eyes were the color of the soft sky after a storm. They loved running, playing, and imagining new adventures together. But sometimes, being different made school harder than they ever expected.

On the first day of school, Zara and Zane felt their hearts race. They had never been to school before! They stepped inside the classroom, their shoes clicking on the floor. All the other kids turned and stared. Some whispered, some giggled, and a few even pointed.

Zara and Zane felt their cheeks turn red. "Why are they looking at us like that?" Zane whispered. Zara squeezed his hand. "Maybe it's because we look different," she said, trying to stay brave. The teacher, Miss Williams, smiled at them warmly. "Welcome, Zara and Zane! You'll make lots of new friends here!"

But as the days passed, Zara and Zane found themselves sitting alone at lunch. The other kids didn't know how to talk to them. Some were scared, others were confused. "Are you sick?" one boy asked. "Why is your skin so white?" another girl wondered. Zara and Zane didn't know what to say. They felt sad, but they didn't want to give up.

One sunny afternoon, Miss Williams called them to the front of the class. "Zara, Zane," she said kindly, "Would you like to share something important with your classmates?" Zara and Zane looked at each other, unsure. "Do you think they'll understand?" Zane whispered. Zara nodded, a little nervous but excited. "Let's tell them the truth!" she said.

Zara stood up first, her hands shaking a little. But when she looked at Zane, his smile gave her courage. "Hi, everyone! We want to tell you something about ourselves," Zara said, her voice a little shaky at first, but then growing stronger. "We have a condition called albinism. It's not a disease. It's just how we were born."

Zane took a deep breath and added, "Albinism means we don't have enough pigment, called melanin, in our skin, hair, and eyes. That's why we look the way we do."

Some kids gasped. "So, you're not sick?" one girl asked.

"No, not at all!" Zane smiled. "We're just like you, with a little extra sunshine inside us!"

Zara's eyes sparkled as she continued. "People with albinism can do everything you can do! We love to play, we love to run, and we love to learn. But our eyes are special, and sometimes we need to wear sunglasses or hats to protect ourselves from the sun. We also see a little differently because of how our eyes work."

Miss Williams clapped her hands together. "Would you like to share more with us, Zara and Zane?"

The twins nodded eagerly, excited to share more.

Here's what they told the class:

- Did you know there are about 1 in 20,000 people with albinism around the world? It's rare, but it happens to people everywhere!

- Albinism is caused by genes passed down from our parents. It's not something you can catch.

- People with albinism often need to wear special glasses or sun protection because of their eyes and skin.

- Albinism doesn't stop us from doing anything! We can play sports, read books, and dream big dreams, just like everyone else.

Suddenly, the classroom was filled with whispers and excited voices. "Wow!" said one boy. "That's so cool!"

"I didn't know that," another girl said, her eyes wide.

From that moment on, things began to change. The kids in class stopped staring and started asking questions—not out of fear, but because they were curious and eager to learn more.

Every day after that, Zara and Zane became more and more confident. The other kids wanted to protect them from the sun, so they started bringing hats and sunscreen to play outside. They even made sure to stand in the shade when it was too bright. "We've got your back!" they said, smiling as they shared their knowledge.

Zara and Zane couldn't believe it. They were finally making friends! One by one, the children in their class began to understand and appreciate how unique and amazing Zara and Zane were. And the twins realized something powerful: They didn't have to hide who they were. By sharing their story, they had turned a challenge into a new beginning.

At recess, Zara and Zane played tag, laughed, and raced around the playground with their new friends. It felt like the world was shining just a little brighter, and they knew—no matter what—being different was something to celebrate.

The sun was setting as Zara and Zane walked home together, hand in hand. "Today was amazing!" Zane said, bouncing along. "I think we really helped them understand."

Zara nodded, her heart swelling with pride. "We sure did. And now we can all shine bright, together!"

Statistics and Facts about Albinism:

1. Prevalence:
Albinism is rare, occurring in approximately 1 in 20,000 to 1 in 40,000 births worldwide. In some parts of Africa, it is more common, occurring in 1 in 1,400 births.

2. Genetic Causes:
Albinism is caused by a genetic mutation that affects melanin production. There are several types, such as Oculocutaneous Albinism (affecting skin, hair, and eyes) and Ocular Albinism (affecting the eyes mostly).

3. Vision Challenges:
People with albinism often experience vision problems, such as difficulty seeing in low light, sensitivity to bright lights, and involuntary eye movements (nystagmus). But with the right tools, like glasses or magnifiers, they can see clearly.

4. Sun Protection:
Because they have little melanin, people with albinism are more sensitive to the sun. They need to wear sunscreen, sunglasses, and protective clothing to avoid sunburn or skin damage.

5. A Global Issue:
Albinism affects people from all ethnicities, but in some regions, people with albinism face greater challenges, including social stigma or even violence, due to myths and misunderstandings.

6. Celebrating Differences:
With education, we can reduce stigma and celebrate the beauty of diversity. People with albinism are strong, vibrant, and capable of achieving incredible things!

www.ingramcontent.com/pod-product-compliance
Lightning Source LLC
LaVergne TN
LVHW060133080526
838201LV00118B/3044